THE TEACHER'S INNOVATION WORKBOOK

THE TEACHER'S INNOVATION WORKBOOK

A Step-by-Step Guide to Planning and Achieving Your Goals

Leah Wasburn-Moses

Rowman & Littlefield
Lanham • Boulder • New York • London

Published by Rowman & Littlefield
A wholly owned subsidiary of The Rowman & Littlefield Publishing Group, Inc.
4501 Forbes Boulevard, Suite 200, Lanham, Maryland 20706
www.rowman.com

Unit A, Whitacre Mews, 26-34 Stannary Street, London SE11 4AB

Copyright © 2018 by Leah Wasburn-Moses

All rights reserved. No part of this book may be reproduced in any form or by any electronic or mechanical means, including information storage and retrieval systems, without written permission from the publisher, except by a reviewer who may quote passages in a review.

British Library Cataloguing in Publication Information Available

Library of Congress Cataloging-in-Publication Data Is Available
ISBN 978-1-4758-3900-5 (pbk: alk. paper)
ISBN 978-1-4758-3901-2 (electronic)

♾️ The paper used in this publication meets the minimum requirements of American National Standard for Information Sciences—Permanence of Paper for Printed Library Materials, ANSI/NISO Z39.48-1992.

Printed in the United States of America

To my first teachers, Philo and Mara, who have always been there for me;

to exceptional dance teachers Ashley and Michael, who encourage me to shoot for the stars in many ways;

and to teachers everywhere who are making a difference every day.

Contents

Introduction 1

Step 1 Outlining Your Project 3

Step 2 Brainstorming 7

Step 3 Setting a Timeline 11

Step 4 Planning for Evaluation 17

Step 5 Creating a Proposal 21

Step 6 Planning and Implementation 25

Step 7 Growth and Development 29

Appendix A: Sample Case 1—High School Reading Course 35

Appendix B: Sample Case 2—Middle-School Gifted Math Intervention 45

Appendix C: Sample Case 3—Alternative School Program 55

Appendix D: Sample Case 4—Arts Enrichment 65

About the Author 73

Introduction

Dear teacher,

By purchasing this workbook, you have taken the first step in accomplishing your goals: goals that will serve you, your school community, and your students. This workbook is for you if you aspire to create something new—a tutoring program, before- or after-school intervention, a partnership with an external group, arts enrichment, and much, much more.

By following the seven steps outlined in this workbook, you will learn to organize and explicate your ideas and convey them to others with clarity, locate outside resources to assist you in your efforts, create a manageable timeline, and build a comprehensive evaluation plan. The step-by-step instructions and fill-in-the-blank format with concrete examples are intended to provide structure and build confidence at each step along the way.

So much of the work you will be doing is grounded in your ability to stay focused, organized, and work through problems. This workbook assists you in organizing your work for your own benefit as well as for presentation to others; aligning goals, plans, and outcomes; and anticipating problems before they occur. It provides blank worksheets for each step along the way, as well as sample cases so you can see the planning for four projects from start to finish.

Each of the sample cases is based on a real-life project initiated by educators. Sample Case 1 involves a high school special educator who creates a credit-bearing class for his struggling readers. Sample Case 2 surrounds a middle-school math teacher who designs an enrichment opportunity for her gifted students. Sample Case 3 is about a middle-school teacher who builds a new position for himself as the teacher of an alternative school classroom. Sample Case 4 involves an elementary school art teacher who initiates a partnership to provide additional opportunities in the arts outside the school day.

As you begin your work, remember to reward yourself at each step along the way. Make sure not to rush yourself—your project must fit your lifestyle, and so must the work leading up to implementation and beyond. Try to be realistic about your goals and your timeline.

Most important, know your strengths and weaknesses and try to incorporate strategies to support yourself. For example, are you a procrastinator? Set deadlines and reward yourself for sticking to them. Have difficulty finding time to work on your project? Set aside a block of time each day or each week and reward yourself for following through.

Organization is another issue to consider. Aside from the work contained in this book, you will need a system to organize planning documents, data, fliers, and more related to your project. An electronic folder, binders, and three-prong folders can all be used to organize your work. Once you start collecting data, you may need to expand your system. You do not want to discard any artifacts related to planning, implementation, or evaluation prematurely. After all, a few years from now, someone may wish to replicate your work.

So, dig in, have fun, and above all, don't forget to have pride in your accomplishments!

Step 1

Outlining Your Project

The ability to communicate your ideas in a succinct and accessible manner is imperative. Therefore, your first step is to identify a working title and a write a one-sentence summary of your project. Later, you will need to form an "elevator speech," whether you need it or not, to explain your ideas to individuals who are stakeholders. Stakeholders are those individuals whose support and/or input is imperative to the success of your project.

The outline worksheet provided in figure 1.1 will assist you in clarifying and defining your project. Once you have clear goals and are able to articulate some of the strengths and challenges associated with implementing your ideas, you will be able to move forward with productive brainstorming. Here is the information you will need to complete the worksheet.

Title: Try for as descriptive a title as possible, in as few words as possible. Your title should be no more than four to five words, e.g., "After-School Writing Tutoring," "Sixth Grade RTI in Mathematics," or "Lunchtime Chess," rather than something catchy, such as "Writing Rangers," "Math 4 Success," or "Chess Challenge." Notice that the sample titles cover some of the "W" questions, such as who, what, and when. Don't abandon your ideas for catchy titles, though, because as you get closer to implementation and a wider variety of individuals become aware of program, you may want to pull these ideas back out to assist you with "advertisement" and recall.

One-sentence summary: The one-sentence summary needs to cover even more of the "W" questions than the title. You need the summary for your own benefit, so you are clear about the scope of the project, and for the benefit of others, so they are able to understand quickly the bottom line, in other words, what you are doing and why. You also want to be somewhat specific about the population. For example, in Sample Case 1 Mr. Wayne is targeting high school students reading at third-grade level or below.

Goal: The goal of your project needs to be as specific as possible. Ideally, you would wish to state, "Raise seventh grade science achievement from 56 percent proficient to 66 percent proficient," but you are not always able to set this kind of precise goal. Instead, you could say, "Improve proficiency scores on x test." Your goal may simply be exposure or participation. If you can tie your goals in to the school or district's stated mission, vision, or goals, consider using that same language as you write your goal statement.

Even though it seems obvious, take a moment to ensure that your goal statement matches your one-sentence summary; that is, your goal (outcome) matches the input you identify earlier. Many of us have finished writing an essay or article only to realize that the ending does not match the initial purpose or theme statement. Ensuring this type of match is important to come back to repeatedly throughout the creative process.

Problem: What problem or need does your project address? What is wrong with current programming? The problem may be a need to raise test scores. If your project can fit into this format, it is a good idea to do so, because it is more likely that school administration will be on board. However, we all know that not all worthwhile programming can be couched in the language of achievement test scores.

The problem may be that the district does not have sufficient opportunities for students in a certain area, such as to engage in creative expression, to participate in intercultural exchanges, or to acquire outdoor survival skills. In the case where there is not clear alignment between your project and district goals or test scores, it may be worthwhile to engage in some basic background research, such as locating statistics relating your project to positive outcomes for youth.

For example, research has linked participation in music and art activities to various positive lifetime outcomes. The same can be said of career/technical education and various extracurriculars, even though they may not be considered "high priority" for many districts. You may want to refer to the need for greater parent engagement or increased morale among the school community. If you do outside research, be sure to cite your source on every document you write, even if informally (e.g., "American Heart Association"). Your stakeholders need to see that you did your homework, and you may need to come back to the source later to do additional research.

Solution: Your solution statement should be a combination of the one-sentence summary and the goal. It may feel redundant, because you are repeating information you have already recorded, but a solution statement is important because it shows the logic directly connecting the problem to your solution.

For example, in Sample Case 2 the summary, goal, and solution all mention increasing achievement and engagement in the area of mathematics through enrichment. In this way, the overall proposal hangs together. The solution is more than the "what," "when," and "where" of your project; however, at this point the statement should be no longer than two to three sentences.

Stakeholders: This section is an opportunity for you to identify who has a "stake" in your project. It is best to cast a wide net in these cases; with many projects the individuals impacted may extend well beyond those who might initially be considered stakeholders. In particular, parents and various school administrators are easy to overlook.

When dealing with a special population, more "levels" of personnel may be involved. For example, Sample Case 2 is about gifted education. In this case, the gifted math teachers and the gifted coordinator are included. Even though they may not be participating in the intervention on a daily basis, they will need to be included in the planning. Also, do not forget students! Many times they are the ultimate stakeholders in an educational project.

Costs: This can be one of the most difficult areas for educators to determine and may take some time and thought. There are obvious costs to programs, such as transportation, salaries, stipends, or materials, but there may also be more hidden costs, such as maintaining a building after hours, keeping an administrator on call, or professional development.

Be sure to identify the source of any cost estimates. Costs are among the first questions you will be asked and are the reason many initiatives are nixed even before they start. Considering costs and planning how to minimize them is important to include among your very first steps.

Issues: Clearly, not all problems can be foreseen. However, if you can anticipate and plan for issues ahead of time, you will be able to move forward with your project more quickly. Many of these issues will be related to cost. Other common issues with new educational programming include student transportation, physical space, and parent permission. Be sure to fill out this section carefully, because the next step, brainstorming, will involve you in leveraging your contacts to find creative solutions to some of these issues.

Chain of approval: From the outset, you will need to know the process you will go through to obtain approval for implementing your project. Sometimes, there is an informal as well as a formal process. For example, you may be expected to ask colleagues for permission to move forward with your project before you approach administrators.

School politics can wreak havoc with a project proposal, so some discreet inquiries can assist (e.g., find out who really makes the decisions and get him or her on board first). It is best if you are able to locate a written policy regarding the proposal approval process. That way, you can refer to the policy to justify your actions.

The chain of approval should also connect with your stakeholder list, although it will not be a 100 percent match. At least one of the individuals on the chain of approval should ideally be a stakeholder or someone impacted by the project, probably as a supervisor. It is important to note, though, that not every "chain of approval" is necessarily a chain. It might simply be one person who has to agree to your project. In that case, you should count yourself lucky and not overthink. If you ask too many people, someone will always say "no."

When you fill out this part of your worksheet, be sure to keep it as simple as possible. For example, in Sample Case 2, the general education teachers whose classes will be impacted need to approve of the intervention first. Then the gifted coordinator will need to check the content before it goes to the principal for final approval. Sample Case 3 has the most complex chain of approval because it actually forms a new school program. It involves transportation and the approval of partners at higher levels, including district and university leadership.

Partner(s): These are individuals, groups, organizations, or businesses who will assist you in implementing your project. You may not need any partners, but you might consider adding them even if they are not crucial to your project. Sometimes, they can take some of the administrative burden and add a new dimension of creativity to your project. Partners will all be stakeholders, but they constitute a smaller group of stakeholders—those whose actions are crucial to your ability to implement your project.

For example, partners might be a business or college supplying mentors; the organization providing materials; or teachers, counselors, or teams recommending appropriate students to participate in your project. Obviously, having appropriate and willing partners is crucial to the success of your project. Although the involvement of partners will vary widely from project to project, the ability to identify partners and rely on their support early on is related to later success.

Evaluation: Evaluation can be simple or complex. You, your partners, your stakeholders, and those in your chain of approval will all need to know how you will determine whether you are meeting (or exceeding) your stated goal(s) and to what extent. This means evaluation must be part of your project from day one.

Evaluation may seem daunting, but it is related directly to your goal and solution statement listed earlier. You will learn more about how to develop and implement your evaluation plan in step 4, but for now it is important to jot down even the most basic thoughts about how you might begin to measure the impact of the project you have planned.

Progress monitoring is important to consider as well because often results are not known for a significant period of time after a project has commenced (e.g., annual test scores, graduation rates). How can you demonstrate that your program is showing initial success, that students are improving their skills, and that students and/or parents are satisfied with your work? Again, more information on evaluation planning is in step 4.

Clearly, you will keep reworking many of the aspects of planning contained in this step. However, before you close the book on it and move to step 2, take some time out to think and get creative with your plans. Where do you do your best thinking and at what time of day? In the shower first thing in the morning? At the gym at noon? In your child's bedroom at night? Take some time to go to this place without any preconceived problems to solve.

The goal is to think generally about your project. Don't pressure yourself and you may be surprised at the creativity that will bubble up to the surface. On the other hand, try not to be discouraged if nothing comes to you. That may be an indicator that you are already on the right track with your project.

Outline Worksheet
Title of project:
One-sentence summary:
Goal
Problem
Solution

- What (two sentences or less)
- When
- Where
- Stakeholders
- Costs

Issues (n/a if not applicable)

- Transportation
- Space
- Parent permission
- Chain of approval
- Partners
- Evaluation (including progress monitoring)

Figure 1.1

Step 2

Brainstorming

You may have thought a lot about your project, and you may even have discussed it with friends, family, and colleagues. Targeted, planned brainstorming will provide you with ideas and opportunities you may not have considered previously. It is important to be strategic and organized when planning for brainstorming. Your outline will help you.

Since only you know your project, you will need to pick and choose who needs to be included in brainstorming, what information these individuals will need to know about your project before providing advice, and what to ask them. Although there will always be some questions, especially quick ones, that you will need to ask others via e-mail, the type of brainstorming presented here should be conducted face-to-face, unless there are extenuating circumstances that preclude this type of session.

First, you will need to determine whether to brainstorm with individuals, with groups, or with both. If you need assistance with major aspects of the project, such as locating a partner or determining the location of the project, it is best to speak individually with people who might best provide advice in each targeted area. Later on, after you have refined your ideas to the extent that you are able to provide a firm response to each of the questions in the outline provided in step 1, you should move to the focus group.

If your plan is very simple, you may not need the focus group. However, focus groups often provide creative solutions to issues and different ways of thinking that can broaden the way you see your project. Your questions to individuals can be less focused and broader (e.g., What should the program look like?), whereas questions you can pose to a group should be quite specific (e.g., What curriculum should I use? How should I advertise my program?), because it is easy for groups to lose focus.

Second, the objectives for the brainstorming session(s) and the questions you ask participating individuals are very important. They should flow directly from the objectives for your project, and they need to hit the "meat" of your project hard. For example, in Sample Case 4, before anyone is going to consent to an after-school art project, he or she must know the costs.

In Sample Case 2, an appropriate curriculum is needed to convince stakeholders that students will be engaged in the proposed math activity. Further, those involved in the focus group will undoubtedly contribute to your knowledge of math curricula and activities, so you will end up with a more creative and better thought-out plan for your project.

Selecting the right individuals to assist with brainstorming is easier than selecting members for a focus group. It is advantageous to include both insiders (e.g., colleagues) and outsiders, even people with little or no knowledge of education. The outsiders will tell you quickly if you need to work on how you explain your project to a lay audience.

The ability to describe your project quickly and easily to outsiders is important because parents, partners, and other community members may need to access information about the project. Some individuals must be selected for a conversation (e.g., you may need to ask your principal for ideas regarding what time during the school day you might offer a writing workshop).

However, for areas in which multiple people might offer advice, try to stick with people who have a "can-do" attitude, as opposed to those who tend to reject new ideas out of hand and explain immediately why they cannot work. You do not want to avoid criticism; in fact, you need it. However, you want to avoid people who tend to provide nothing but criticism.

The advantage of the focus group is that ideas can build from others' comments in ways in which you are not able to anticipate. Selecting individuals to participate in focus groups can be challenging, because you want to ensure that this dynamic will result in positive outcomes for you. Depending on what issues you are targeting, you may wish to invite one representative from each stakeholder group (e.g., parent, teacher, administrator, community partner), or you may wish to invite diverse people who all bring the same type of expertise to the table (e.g., a team of math teachers to advise you about a tutoring curriculum).

Consider when in the planning process you want to bring partners into the picture. There are some partners you might not want to include when you are "letting it all hang out," that is, bringing forward multiple issues or otherwise showing how little of the project you have planned thus far. Regardless of the stage of planning process, before setting up any focus group, you must have a clear vision of what you want to ask/learn from the group, as well as who is most appropriate to include in the group.

If you are not yet able to provide that vision and/or make that determination, you might want to stick with brainstorming with individuals until you are able to meet this standard. Of course, these sessions might include some of the same people, which has its advantages and disadvantages.

Writing objectives for the brainstorming session and putting them down on paper (Brainstorming Worksheet) might help you get started planning. If you are planning on using both individual and group brainstorming, you may need to write separate objectives. Once you write the objectives, questions for the brainstorming meeting(s) should follow directly and be a good match.

For example, Sample Case 3 involves meeting with individuals at two different entities, a school district and a university. Some questions are the same for each group and some differ. You may not want the two partners to get together until you have hashed out some details. In this case, Mr. Meade needed to determine the correct youth population, and he needed to determine which college students would be serving as tutors and mentors. It made sense to ask these questions of leadership at the district and college separately rather than posing it to a mixed group. Once he had the proposed populations, he was ready to meet together to determine what scheduling might look like. Sample Case 4 is similar, in that Ms. Sims needed to meet with stakeholders at the school and at the Local Arts Center.

Consider carefully the materials you provide to a group. Both the content and questions should fit easily on one piece of paper. Look back at the outline you produced for step 1. What elements of this outline constitute crucial knowledge for your focus group so that they can understand what they need of your project and apply their expertise to assist you in planning?

When creating an agenda, always start with your objectives for the session and be sure to include some kind of timetable, even if that is simply listing the targeted implementation date. You might also need to bring some reference materials with you. For example, in Sample Case 2, materials include summaries of potential curricula. The work that Ms. Gilbert has completed ahead of time will help her use her time more wisely in the brainstorming session, because she is not relying on her focus group members to determine potential curricula on the spot for her to consider later. Instead, they are selecting one as a group during the session.

With respect to communicating your ideas in a small space, an outline or other visual aid can be superior to simple text, because it is easier to follow and understand. For ideas about different types of graphic organizers that can assist you in organizing your ideas, Google "Holt Interactive Graphic Organizers," and you will find more than enough choices. Another consideration when planning a focus group is the venue. You should find a place that is quiet and away from distractions, but is also comfortable and accessible.

When crafting questions for brainstorming, many people write questions that are too general and that can lead the group off task. If your questions are more general (e.g., What type of art projects should I use? What population of students should I target?), you should pose fewer questions to allow more time to be spent in this one area. If your questions are more specific (e.g., What time during the school day should I offer my new course?), you can pose fewer questions to the group.

Consider sending your agenda to your group ahead of time so you can hit the ground running, although do not assume your group members will all do their reading ahead of time. The location for your brainstorming session(s) is also important. Select a location that is accessible and relaxed, although away from distractions. Mark the time and location you chose on the worksheet.

Since it is unlikely that everyone in the focus group will be close friends or colleagues who are willing to take time just to assist you, I recommend providing some kind of thank-you reward, such as snacks, a boxed meal (for longer sessions or those scheduled during lunch), or even a $5 gift card to Starbucks. This way, without spending much money, your participants will work harder to help you and walk away with positive feelings about the group and your ideas. The knowledge that they assisted you in starting something new will stick with them. They will also be more likely to support your project if they are stakeholders and feel as though they had some input into the initial planning.

Finally, when planning brainstorming sessions, do not forget to consider asking your focus group for assistance locating grant opportunities and planning for evaluation. These are areas in which the average educator lacks expertise. However, there are people working in and affiliated with schools who are very knowledgeable in each of these areas.

Innovation does not mean learning everything about every possible aspect of your project. It does mean being able to locate individuals who do know about each aspect and making good use of them by getting to know them, communicating to them that you value their knowledge and input, asking the right questions, and rewarding them for their efforts, even if just a simple "thank-you."

When you lead groups of people, there are more issues to consider than when you are just meeting with one individual. During the group session, you are the moderator. Do not be afraid to butt in! You will need to set ground rules first, and then stick to them. Common ground rules are to avoid negativity (e.g., saying something cannot be done or cutting someone else off with a reason of why their idea will not work), staying away from technology distractions, and avoiding side conversations.

You may wish to include this list on the materials you provide ahead of time, or wait until the meeting itself. Regardless, the rules should be visible to all participants at all times during the meeting. Do not be afraid to refer to them, either. Be prepared with chart paper and/or a person to take notes so you get everything down at the time and then organize your thoughts later.

Brainstorming Worksheet

Choice of formats: individual ☐   group ☐   both ☐

Justification for choice of formats:

Preparation checklist

☐ Prepare written materials (e.g., agenda, timetable)

☐ Identify time and location of meeting(s) _____

☐ Objectives (list below)

    1.

    2.

    3.

☐ Questions you want to be answered

    1.

    2.

    3.

    4.

    5.

☐ Locate thank-you gift _____

☐ Write ground rules (for focus groups only)

    1.

    2.

    3.

☐ List all materials (e.g., copies, chart paper, markers)

    1.

    2.

    3.

    4.

Step 3

Setting a Timeline

Setting a timeline is as important for stakeholders as it is for you. Both need to see your commitment to the project, and for you, the timeline can serve as an effective motivator. One of the first aspects to consider is the correct unit for your timeline—typically, weeks or months. People tend to be unrealistic about timelines, by underestimating both the amount of time it will take them and others to complete assigned tasks and the amount of time it will take for approval processes. Be sure to keep these tips in mind as you complete your timeline (see Box 3.1).

Start with the preliminary timeline shown in Box 3.1. To begin this timeline, start with the implementation date and work backward. Your first worksheet in this step asks you to identify the implementation date (by week, month, or year). Note that this particular timeline is considered a planning timeline, in that it ends at implementation. You will create more timelines as you get deeper into this project; these timelines are presented in steps 6 and 7.

Many educational projects need to commence at the beginning of the semester; when in doubt, move the start date back a semester to ensure sufficient time for approvals and planning. After you have identified the implementation date, attempt to identify each of the tasks you will need to complete before implementation. These are major tasks that are crucial to the success of your project.

Looking at Sample Case 1, Mr. Wayne must identify the curriculum and students. However, purchasing gifts for the brainstorming meeting and sending a reminder note home to participating students could be considered details, and should not be included yet. In Sample Case 2, conducting the brainstorming session is a major task, but locating materials for the session and contacting potential team members are minor tasks.

You may wish to write a separate list of minor tasks to put aside for later. At this point, you will have a simple, unordered list of tasks to complete. No detail is too small to be included on this list, such as ordering snacks, collecting permission slips, or locating nametags. These tasks can always be combined later under a larger umbrella term, such as "purchasing items for an opening meeting."

Once you have completed the activity list, set it aside for at least a day to determine what activities you may have missed. Refer back to your outline to ensure a match with what you have planned. Be sure to include details related to any kick-off events, meetings with individuals or focus groups, the approval process, obtaining classroom materials, transportation, parent permissions, evaluation activities, grant-writing, and obtaining space. These are just a few activities that are easy to overlook during the planning process.

The next step is to determine the appropriate unit for your timeline, typically in weeks or months. If your estimated implementation date is less than three months away, your timeline should be in weeks. If your estimated implementation date is between four and six months away, your timeline can be in weeks or months, depending on the number of items on your to-do list and your own organizational preferences. If the date is more than six months away, you should use months as your unit of measure.

Box 3.1

Preliminary Timeline Worksheet

Target implementation date: _____

Major tasks list

    1.

    2.

    3.

    4.

    5.

    6.

    7.

    8.

    9.

    10.

Note that not every space should be full. For example, Sample Case 3 is the most complex and has a twelve-month timeline. Having some blank weeks can give you extra time to complete certain tasks if not everything goes according to plan. For example, Mr. Meade gave himself a "free month" after submitting proposals and checking locations for his program, because he anticipated that these major tasks might incur delays.

If your unit of measure is months and you find that each month has more than three tasks assigned to it, you may wish to switch your timeline to weeks. Different timeline formats are provided at the end of step 2 (see Figures 3.1a, b, and c). Try one and see if it works for you; if not, you can always switch to another format. Additional online timeline templates can be found by Googling "free timeline templates," or you can use a free template on Microsoft Word or PowerPoint.

If you select another format for your timeline, it should include activities or goals, and person(s) included or responsible for overseeing each activity or ensuring its completion. The amount of detail you include on the timeline itself is up to you. Some people like a very simplistic timeline, and some prefer to see more details, such as where and when.

You can also use a timeline that includes space for notes, in order to include those details. For example, in Sample Case 2, Ms. Gilbert needs to "complete logistics" before the end of school. Underneath this entry in her timeline, she lists three minor tasks that need to be completed that she has chosen to group under one header. You may wish to print out multiple copies and place them where you can see them daily as a motivator/reminder.

The next step is to order the list of activities you identified as necessary to implement your project. Again, be sure to plan for extra time. As you begin matching activities to the weeks or months indicated on your timeline, consider your work and personal schedules. You may want to assign fewer (or no) tasks to weeks in which you anticipate greater work, travel, and/or family commitments.

Ask yourself whether the amount of work you have assigned yourself and others is doable; if not, you may need to push back your implementation date. Rushed implementation can lead to omission of details, lack of organization, and less-than-optimal results, not to mention increased stress for yourself and others. Better a later implementation date than rushed implementation.

Finally, go back and check your timeline one more time. If you have assigned tasks to others, are you sure they have sufficient time? Partners are doing you a favor, so you definitely do not want to rush them, even if you are willing to put forth significant personal effort to ensure your project is implemented well and on time.

Also, how can you check to make sure they have completed their assigned task(s)? Take another look at any meetings that are on your timeline. Are you sure the individuals and/or groups named will be able to meet with you within the specified time frame? You must rely on others for at least part of your implementation, but you do not want to create additional stress with setting a timeline that does not accommodate others' schedules.

If you have checked each of the aforementioned items, put your final timeline aside for at least two days to ensure that you have considered all of the details you need to include. Show it to at least two people who know you well, such as one colleague and one close friend or family member, as for their advice regarding whether you can meet the deadlines indicated. They know your personality and work habits, as well as the daily demands on your time. Be sure to consider their recommendations carefully, especially as people tend to overcommit on projects about which they are passionate.

| Timeline #1 |||
Date			
	Task:
	Where:
	Who:
	Notes:
	Task:
	Where:
	Who:
	Notes:
	Task:
	Where:
	Who:
	Notes:
	Task:
	Where:
	Who:
	Notes:

Timeline #2		
January	Major tasks	Minor tasks4
February		
March		
April		
May		
June		

Figure 3.1a, b, and c

Timeline #3

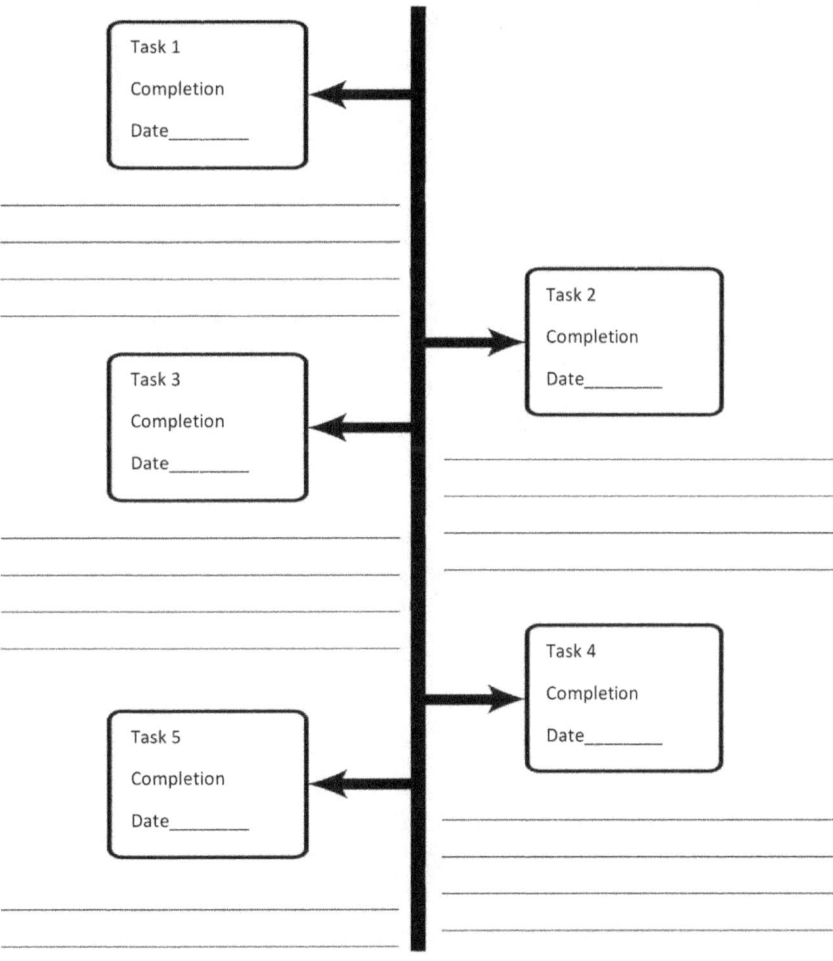

Figure 3.1a, b, and c Continued

Step 4

Planning for Evaluation

A solid evaluation plan is a key to success for any program that provides human services. It will help you stay on track and allows you to defend and share your work with others. Some educators are intimidated by the thought of the evaluation plan because it may conjure up thoughts of intimidating words such as "research" and "statistics." However, don't forget that as an educator you use evaluation every single day in the classroom, and this is no different. Try to keep in mind that the evaluation plan flows naturally from the work you are doing and should not be thought of as a separate entity.

Figure 4.1 shows an evaluation worksheet. In general, you should start by copying your formal goal(s) for your program directly from your outline (e.g., improving reading achievement in sixth-grade students) and then double-check to make sure they are measurable.

In some cases, you will find that the formal goal you set may not be specific enough, particularly if progress in your area is challenging to measure. For example, in Sample Case 4, "develop artistic skill and expression" is a sufficient goal for planning and even for a proposal to share with others, but if you are an art teacher seeking to evaluate student work, you know you will need to dig deeper.

In this case, Ms. Sims chose to select an academic standard from her state in the visual arts in order to rewrite her goal, and then she was able to obtain a rubric in order to measure this goal, developed by her local college. Using an academic standard here can also be helpful, because undoubtedly others have developed assessments and rubrics around that standard. You want this chart to be as simple as possible. For example, in Sample Case 2, there are only two goals, increasing classroom engagement and increasing mathematics achievement. Those can be measured rather simply in ways that will be understood by others.

Although Ms. Gilbert certainly wants to increase creativity and critical thinking, and enhance accelerated learning, these goals are secondary and more difficult to measure.

In Sample Case 3, the only goal is to improve credit attainment. Although this seems like the most simple evaluation plan with only one goal, notice that the plan also requires a comparison group. If you are working with a small number of students, identifying a comparison group can help you demonstrate progress. Be sure to select students for the comparison group carefully. They should have characteristics as close as possible to the group receiving your intervention. In this case, Mr. Meade can choose students who were nominated for the program but chose not to participate.

However, not all goals can be this concrete, as discussed earlier. You may wish to consider adding an "informal" goal, such as providing an engaging after-school program or improving appreciation of various music genres. An informal goal is by definition more difficult to measure, because it often refers to individuals' perceptions rather than something more concrete such as test scores. You do not need to include two goals, one formal and one informal, if it does not fit your project, but you will need to determine how to measure each of the goals you choose to include.

It is easier to cut stated goals later rather than add them in, that is, a clear recipe for your project to become disconnected. You want to be able to show both short- and long-term progress toward the goal(s) you selected through the data that you will be collecting.

The next column is "possible outcomes." This is an opportunity to define what you are looking for a bit more fully. Extending our initial example of improving reading achievement through an after-school program for struggling sixth-grade readers, the outcomes related to the formal goal might include improved grades, improved reading fluency scores, and/or fewer students identified as qualifying for Tier 2 remediation.

The informal goal of providing an engaging program might have possible outcomes of consistent student attendance in the program, feelings of satisfaction with the program, and/or positive views toward reading in school and/or for leisure.

You may have multiple possible outcomes for each of your goals, but you want to ensure that each of the outcomes relates directly to content included in your original outline, typically in the sections covering the problem and solution. Be sure that the possible outcomes flow directly from goals.

The most challenging column for many is locating data sources. When considering how to fill in this column, start with the "easier" sources, the ones that flow directly from the formal goals. For example, a goal of improving third graders' writing might be linked directly to their standardized tests scores in this area. However, such tests are often administered only once per year.

You might wish to identify another test you can administer before, during, and after your intervention to provide more data. In this case, you might use sample writing prompts from your state's standardized test preparation guide, or you might use a portfolio assessment accompanying your curriculum. Many publishers and states post practice tests online that you can use.

Regardless of whether the goal is formal or informal, it is a good idea to use someone else's tests, surveys, or other instrumentation, as in the example in the previous paragraph. Using publicly available materials lends validity to your work. You may not be able to find appropriate instruments to measure every possible outcome that you identify, but you should be able to come close.

As you are listing data sources, make a note as to which ones you will need to use as both pre-tests and post-tests so you can compare scores. For example, you could use a math anxiety instrument as a pre-test and post-test. On the other hand, an instrument designed to measure engagement in an after-school program cannot be given before the program starts, unless you are planning to improve on a preexisting program.

When you are listing data sources, be sure to consider data your school may be already collecting, such as standardized test scores, progress-monitoring scores, or school climate surveys. Using data collected for other purposes lightens your assessment load as well as underscores the connection between your project goals and the goals of your school or district.

Be sure to ask what data is collected in your area of interest, because you may not know everything the school collects from parents or students in various classes. Curriculum specialists, school psychologists, and other administrators may be able to assist you because of their broad knowledge in this area.

Locating outside instruments can be challenging, but there are quite a few websites that can assist with this progress. Try not to make up your own survey instruments or select one that was created by an individual and posted online, because those have not been validated. National organizations such as state education agencies, universities, and subject-matter education groups can have helpful references.

Some recommended online repositories of instruments that may be relevant to your work are listed:

1. Online Evaluation Resource Library, oerl.sri.com
2. University of Kansas Community Toolbox, http://ctb.ku.edu/en
3. Victoria State Government Assessment Tools, http://www.education.vic.gov.au/school/teachers/support/pages/tools.aspx
4. Character.org "School Assessments," http://character.org/more-resources/assessment-tools/school/
5. National Center on Student Progress Monitoring Resources (click on "Progress Monitoring Tools")
6. University of Wisconsin-Stout Rubrics for Assessment, http://www.uwstout.edu/soe/profdev/rubrics.cfm

Be sure not to select lengthy instruments or instruments with more than one to two open-ended questions. If you are looking for in-depth responses, such as if you have few participants and it will be difficult to demonstrate outcomes, or change is otherwise difficult to show, an interview might work better than a survey that requires participants to do a significant amount of writing.

Also, take another moment to consider the fit between the survey instrument and goals. This fit must be tight, and the relationship must be clear to outsiders, or else you are not measuring what you want to measure, and you will need to keep looking for more relevant instruments. The final column addresses the logistics of data collection. How, when, and where can this data be measured/collected?

Too much data is better than too little data, because although you do not have to report all the data you collect, you cannot go back in time and collect additional data. However, you do not want to overwhelm your participants or other stakeholders (e.g., parents, program administrators). Not all data needs to be collected during the time in which you are actually running your program, and others can help you with collection.

As you look at the chart you have created, consider whether you will need everything you have written. Your evaluation plan does need to consider various aspects of your project, but it should also be simple and easy to follow. Again, it should be obvious to an outsider why you have selected your data sources and the connection of those sources to the program goal(s).

Ask for assistance with your evaluation plan. As mentioned earlier, some school personnel know more about collecting, interpreting, and evaluating data than others, such as curriculum specialists, school psychologists, and certain administrators. They might even suggest different ways of collecting and recording your data. Regardless, before you implement your project, you must have a solid handle on what data you need to collect, when it will be collected, and how it will be used.

Finally, before you collect any data, be sure to inquire about your district's policy on research. Collecting data from people is called "research involving human subjects." If the research you are doing is with children, they are considered a protected class because of their vulnerability. Therefore, you will need to be even more careful about how you collect and present your data. At the very least, you will want to share your evaluation plan with the school community, and you want to be able to share it with the wider local or education community at some point.

Sharing data brings up important issues of confidentiality, even if names are never shared. Your school may have a policy whereby parent permission is necessary before certain data can be collected and shared. You do not want to be placed in a position where you are prohibited from reporting the data you collected or, worse, where you are in trouble with administration for collecting or reporting the data you have.

Playing by the rules is very important in this area. You will also need to follow general rules of confidentiality, such as reporting data as a summary and never reporting any data in which an individual student could be identified (e.g., reporting scores by gender when there are only two girls in the group). As you move forward with your proposal, keep coming back to your evaluation plan to ensure that it covers all major aspects of your project.

Evaluation Worksheet			
Goals	Possible Outcomes	Data Sources	Logistics

Figure 4.1

Step 5

Creating a Proposal

This step is perhaps the most important—finalizing a proposal to share with individuals who have decision-making power over your project. These people will play a role in determining whether and under what conditions you will be able to turn your vision into a reality. You want to present sufficient information so an outsider could understand what you are proposing (in fact, sharing it with a family member and/or friend is recommended to assess the accessibility of your writing), but you do not want to overwhelm your readers with detail. In general, your goal with the proposal is to present your project in a concise and clear manner, to stay positive and goal-oriented but to avoid glossing over issues.

Before you approach the writing of the proposal itself, create an "elevator speech"—that is, the major points about your project that you would wish to convey in a thirty-second elevator ride with the person (real or fictional) who has complete control over whether you are able to implement your project. You may write it out as a thirty-second "speech," or you may use bullet points (see notes for "Elevator Speech"). Refer to this speech when you are crafting your proposal to be sure that you have addressed all of these major points.

The proposal should be no more than one page in length, with plenty of blank space. The use of small font and small margins in order to achieve the one-page limit is not recommended. The first worksheet after the "elevator sheet" space depicts a bare-bones proposal format that includes only the required proposal elements discussed here. These are elements that should be contained in any proposal.

Be sure to include your name, title, and contact information as well. Bullet points, numbered lists, and/or ordered outlines are recommended to increase reading ease. Using a plain, no-frills business template, such as those that are included in Word, is acceptable, but fancy fonts or colors are not.

First, fill in all of the required elements listed in the worksheet. Respond as succinctly as possible to leave room for additional elements that will be needed to tailor the proposal to your specific situation. Use tales and charts where possible to increase accessibility and decrease wordiness (e.g., timetable, evaluation). Go back and check each of the previous worksheets you have completed to ensure a match.

Do not worry if goals or details have changed since you first started making notes on your outline; you just want to ensure that all details are up to date, and each section of your proposal works together and adds up to what you envision as your project. Required elements begin with the title of your project, which you may have updated to better reflect the changes you have undoubtedly been making through the process, and a two- to three-sentence overview that states simply what your project will be (e.g., Third-grade Saturday music ensemble at Community Center).

Be sure to start with the problem so readers can see immediately what you are trying to address. For example, in Sample Case 1, Mr. Wayne begins with a concrete statement, the percentage of students he works with who are multiple grade levels below benchmark in reading.

Under Logistics, you will want to respond to the basic "W" questions. Who is the population you are targeting? What is the intervention? When will it take place? You may use sentence format or write out your responses in Q&A format (e.g., "What? After-school reading intervention"). Try to be as specific as possible. Under Evaluation, either write a two- to three-sentence summary of your plan, or provide a bulleted list or abbreviated chart, similar to the one you just completed.

Your timeline is next; again, it will be an abbreviated version of the timeline you just completed. Your timeline will look good in chart format. This is one of the places the approving individual or team will check to determine whether the project is feasible. Finally, communicating next steps in planning is designed to cue your reader that this is where they come in, as stakeholders and/or someone whose assistance you will need as you move forward with planning and implementation.

Next Steps can be written as a list or as a timeline, but you do not want to overwhelm by including all the small details. Balance is necessary in terms of providing the large picture while simultaneously convincing the reader(s) that you have a good handle on detail as well.

Next, compare this basic proposal to your initial outline and to your "elevator speech." What elements are missing that either grab someone's attention as to the potential benefits of your project or are necessary to explain your work? Take a look at the worksheet's Optional Elements. You want to be able to answer the first questions your reader will ask about your project through the proposal. Of course, you cannot anticipate everyone's reaction, but there are certainly questions school administrators, for example, will want to know immediately about a proposed project, such as the following:

1. How much will this project cost the school?
2. How are students going to be transported to and/or from the program?
3. Who will be responsible for the students during the program?
4. Who will oversee the program?
5. Why is this program needed?
6. How will the project contribute to the school's goals (particularly with respect to test scores)?
7. What other commitments will the school need to make (e.g., space, time, materials)?
8. What liabilities might the project encounter?

If there are any costs at all, those must be included in the proposal. For example, Sample Case 4 involves a project that will cost parents $70 for ten sessions. Ms. Sims has included costs under both "Cost to Parents" and "Challenges," because she would like to obtain assistance for parents who have financial need.

Share your proposal with two types of people—friends and family, who have nothing to do with the project, and colleagues who know the environment in which the project will take place. Ask them for feedback in three areas: (1) form, (2) clarity, and (3) content. You may want to hold another focus group session, depending on the importance of the proposal, that is, whether it is just for you to clarify the project to yourself or whether important decisions will be made by others on the basis of the proposal.

At this point, after revisions have been made and your one-pager has been finalized, determine who needs to see the proposal and what the approval process will look like for you to obtain permission to implement your project. This system will vary widely based on the project you have proposed, your professional relationship with the decision maker(s), and the bureaucratic structure of your school or workplace.

You will likely need to translate the proposal you just completed into official forms/documentation provided by your school, but using the format recommended in this book will ensure that all necessary information makes its way onto your "official" proposal. You will also have additional information at the ready in case there are questions or other follow-up requirements you may need to meet.

Partnerships can be quite difficult to navigate at this stage, but remember that it has been done before. The reason why partnerships are particularly tricky is that there may be two approval systems, and those systems never seem to fit well together in terms of approval processes, timelines, or expected documentation. The best course of action is to ask an insider friend at each partnering institution, if you have one, to help you determine how the systems can be made to work together.

Few proposals can be considered simultaneously by two bodies—each tends to like to know that the other one has signed on first, even though it is not possible to do so. Typically, starting with your own workplace is recommended, because you have more to lose if you step on toes inside your own workplace.

Remember, partnerships can work very well, but they have to be approached carefully. You simply may need to resign yourself to learning from your mistakes as you go. It never hurts to say "I'm sorry" or to claim ignorance of the system (also true).

Sample Case 3 is a partnership between a school district and a university. In this case, Mr. Meade chose to put the optional categories "Costs" and "Challenges" in his formal proposal. He chose to include costs because partners expressed significant concern about the potential costs of a new program. He added challenges because he wanted to be up front with partners about their role in setting up a new program, which is a significant undertaking. For example, he was relying on Local U to locate a classroom for him, and he was relying on the district to determine how to provide transportation.

Notes for "Elevator Speech"

Proposal

Title of project: _____

Your name: _____

Date: _____

Brief overview (one to two sentences)

Logistics
- Who?
- What?
- When?
- Where?
- How?

Evaluation:
Timeline:
Next steps:

Optional Proposal Elements
- A. Justification
- B. Goals
- C. Problem
- D. Solution
- E. Costs
- F. Partners
- G. Challenges
- H. Costs
- I. Permission needed
- J. Supplies
- K. Target population

Step 6

Planning and Implementation

Congratulations! Your project is almost ready to go. During the planning phase, arguably the most important element of the work you have completed is the timeline. Again, put your timeline where you can see it, and know yourself. How specific do you need to get with your timeline to make sure the tasks are completed?

If you need to break down tasks into fifteen-minute chunks and write down exactly when you will complete each chunk, do it. If you need a very specific reward system (e.g., thirty minutes of Netflix for one hour of work, no snack until thirty minutes of devoted work time), do it. Get your family in on it as well—they'll help you stick to your goals.

This is a good time to consider carefully the "official" name of your project. At first, you were counseled to select a name that was very down-to-earth and descriptive. However, now you are going for a title that is a bit catchier. You still want to say something about your project in its title. For example, you generally want to avoid a title like "Blue Dragons," which says nothing about form, content, or target audience, but you do have permission to get a little bit creative at this stage.

In Sample Case 2, the title changes from "Mathematics Enrichment for Gifted Students," which is descriptive and will make more sense on an initial proposal, to "Math Break!" which will engage students and parents. It is difficult to anticipate the future of the project at this point, so be sure you are totally satisfied with the name before you move forward with it. Often, friends, family, and colleagues can be very helpful in assisting you in naming your work.

You may find that you need to adjust your timeline throughout this phase, and you will need to take what seems like a setback as a matter of course. Sometimes you will have been able to build in setbacks to your timeline (e.g., approval processes take longer than anticipated, focus group cannot meet on the week indicated on the timeline), but obviously many setbacks, such as illness, family emergencies, or snow days cannot be anticipated. Although it is difficult to be forced to inform your supervisors and/or other stakeholders that your project cannot commence when originally intended, again, better a well-put-together project that starts later than anticipated than one that is rushed and poorly implemented.

As your implementation deadline approaches, you will need to extend your timeline beyond the point of implementation. The timeline you created in step 3 was a planning timeline; that is, it only took you up to the moment your project would be implemented. Now you need to think past implementation to evaluation, growth, and development. What you learn in this step and the next step will assist you in creating that timeline.

Include all aspects of the evaluation plan in this extended timeline, as well as some plans for dissemination. Without compromising your evaluation plan (it is likely you will need to do some initial data collection), you want to give yourself some time to get your feet wet with your new project before you really begin digging into evaluation and dissemination efforts, and plans for growth and development.

Undoubtedly, your time will be spent "putting out fires," dealing with unexpected issues, and you want to take the time to gain some perspective on the project itself and what it looks like in reality as opposed to just on paper before you begin planning for its future. You may be surprised (hopefully pleasantly) about the differences between theory, or the plans you wrote, and what your project looks like in reality.

At this stage, it is easy to become disorganized. You may not have time to stay organized and keep track of all the notes, materials, deadlines, paperwork, and so on that may be accumulating rapidly. If you do not have time to organize, throw everything into a desk drawer and/or computer file to sort through later. Anecdotal data, that is, notes about the project's logistics, participants, and so on, can be very useful later on. You may not have time to look at your pretest scores or informal evaluation results, but be sure to take time to clip responses together so they do not get separated. Post-it notes can be helpful when you are in a hurry, in terms of allowing you to clip, label, dump, and go.

It can be very difficult to sort everything out later if you cannot remember what something is, when it was collected, or from whom it was collected. Everything should be saved, including lesson plans, unsolicited feedback (e.g., e-mails from parents, teachers, or administrators), attendance rosters, and used materials. You can always have a recycling binge when you are certain you have no need for something later on.

Again, it is difficult to plan for setbacks, but you can do more than just give yourself extra time on your timeline. You need to plan for extra thinking time alone, and brainstorming with stakeholders, colleagues, and/or friends, depending on the issue and its sensitivity. Never make an immediate decision that changes your program dramatically unless absolutely necessary (e.g., transportation does not show up and you decide to switch to parent transport for the day). You want to keep the integrity of the project until such time as you can make a reasoned, informed decision to change it.

If possible, involve colleagues in the first few days of implementation of your project to obtain preliminary feedback and to gain personal and professional support, as well as to assist you if issues arise that require your immediate attention. Schedule in some time for yourself if possible, doing what you need to do to relax. If you can, ask others to take over some tasks for you temporarily while you adjust to the stresses of the implementation phase.

Once you have gotten your feet wet and feel as though you have some basic perspective on your project, you should begin thinking about preliminary dissemination. You will want to ensure that you are able to provide information on both short- and long-term success. In the short term, you will need to cultivate awareness about and positive feelings toward your project.

The most important first step is to keep your administrator or other immediate supervisor informed about the progress of your project. Even a two-sentence e-mail reminds him or her about the existence of the project and demonstrates your organization and commitment. As soon as you have any data at all, be sure to send that in an accessible format.

Even simple attendance numbers, parental permissions received, funds raised, or materials donated can be communicated in a positive way that makes an impact with higher-ups. Once you have more solid data, such as that from progress-monitoring and/or satisfaction surveys, you want to be sure to send a summary to your stakeholders as soon as possible. People like good news, and they like to feel involved in innovation.

Although we educators are not accustomed to bragging about our work, now is not the time to be shy. The more people who know about your project and who have a positive attitude toward it, the more difficult it is for someone to cancel the project. With this information in mind, pick some easy targets first. Perhaps you can invite a school administrator to visit, as well as a higher-up in any partnering organization. Your school newsletter or student paper could write about the project.

You can volunteer to present a five-minute overview of your project at a faculty meeting. Include data in a visible and accessible format where possible. All of these ideas are low-stake, easy-to-implement activities that will gain you the recognition you deserve, as well as cultivate support as you move forward to the next stage of your project.

Step 7

Growth and Development

Once you feel comfortable with your project, the fires have been out, you have some preliminary data that shows success, and your project is integrated in the school community, you are ready for step 7, growth and development. As you already know, if you do not stay current as an educator, tend to your own professional development, and change things up in the classroom, your teaching will stagnate and you will quickly become a good candidate for burnout. Even if you are completely satisfied with your project, there is always room for some type of growth.

Even before you begin to consider growth, you need to address self-sufficiency and plan for the continuation of your project as it currently stands. If you are relying on some type of funding in order to operate, considering how to ensure your funding is extended is the first order of business. For example, the growth and development plan for Sample Case 4 includes locating a donor to provide art supplies on an ongoing basis.

However, self-sufficiency is about more than just funds. Does the project rely too heavily on you? You want the project to be able to continue to exist even if for some reason you were not there to administer it. Can you rely on student or parent helpers to shoulder some of the administrative burden? How can you make administration simpler? What does it take to keep your project running? How do you prepare for each session? Take some time to fill the blank sheet provided with list of tasks, calendar, or chart that depicts the organization of administration of your project.

Second, how can you promote this project both within and outside the school community? Again, the more people know about and support your project, the more difficult it is for administrators and others to decide it should be discontinued. Be sure to use the name of your project in every communication. Ask for project updates to appear in school newsletters and other print and electronic communication sent to parents and the broader community. Then save the results, whether electronic or hard copy.

Consider using social media to send updates such as student accomplishments, parent praises, publicity, or special events. Get your local newspaper or television involved. Even if you think your project is too small for local media, it does not hurt to try, and you might be surprised. Local media often look for positive anecdotes to include in their press, especially related to the accomplishments of and opportunities for young people in the community.

Submit brief articles, including data summaries, to district and state education newsletters for potential publication. Consider any education organizations to which you belong. Once you write one blurb, it is easy to send it to multiple outlets. You may even have a media or communications person at your building who can assist you in these efforts.

Third, when you are ready to begin planning for the second semester or second year of your project, begin to consider future expansion in addition to any changes you might like to make in the project's structure. For example, could you take more students? Use more space? Meet twice instead of once a week? Have students enter a local contest or display or present their work publicly? Incorporate community trips? The sample cases presented cover each of these contingencies. Often, students themselves are the best ambassadors for your project and can provide creative input with respect to its future. These types of changes increase the impact as well as the visibility of your project.

Jot down an informal list of future goals for your project underneath your notes on administration. Be sure to keep in mind the three tenets, stability, quality, and self-sufficiency. Nothing is too grand for the list—do not rule out expansion to other sites in a few years' time. The more you can demonstrate that your project is easy to set up and administer, and shows positive results, the more attractive it will be to other schools and organizations.

At this point, it may be impossible to connect the dots on a timeline, but why not mark down a five- or ten-year goal that includes your own building, additional sites, more partners, or expansion grants? This is the time to get creative and to get ambitious. You can worry about the details and what is a reasonable versus unreasonable goal as you continue to learn more about how your project works. Sometimes if powerful players get on board, such as a superintendent or community leader, that person can move mountains for you. Figures 7.1 a and b depict two formal Growth and Development plans to help guide your work.

Be sure not to skip over data collection and analysis. It is easy to gloss over these tasks when you are in the midst of implementation—planning for your next session, rounding up snacks, dealing with transportation—or have supervised a project for a number of years. However, if data collection and analysis are not happening on a regular basis as planned, you will have little to show the outside world regarding all your hard work. You want to depict your data in an accessible format, using charts and graphs to compare pre-tests and post-tests and display other information.

Remember to follow your institution's rules for research. If you are careful, you can present and publish this data to get the word out about your project in the education community. Consider what your subject area association has to offer. Here are a few organizations that might be a good fit, depending on your subject/grade:

- Alliance for Health, Physical Education, Recreation, and Dance (AAHPDERD), shapeamerica.org
- American Council on the Teaching of Foreign Language (ACTFL), actfl.org
- Association for Middle Level Education (AMLE), amle.org
- Council for Exceptional Children (CEC), cec.sped.org
- International Reading Association (IRA), literacyworldwide.org
- International Society for Technology in Education (ISTE), iste.org
- National Art Education Association (NAEA), naea-reston.org
- National Association for Gifted Children (NAGC), nagc.org
- National Association for Music Education (NafME), nafme.org
- National Association for the Education of Young Children (NAEYC), naeyc.org
- National Council for the Social Studies (NCSS), socialstudies.org
- National Council of Teachers of English (NCTE), ncte.org
- National Council of Teachers of Mathematics (NCTM), nctm.org

Organizational Structure

Name of project: _____

Future goals

1.

2.

3.

32 / Step 7

Growth and Development Plan #1

Project title:

Goal	Tasks	Targeted Completion Date	Notes
Goal	Tasks	Targeted Completion Date	Notes
Goal	Tasks	Targeted Completion Date	Notes
Goal	Tasks	Targeted Completion Date	Notes
Goal	Tasks	Targeted Completion Date	Notes

Growth and Development Plan #2

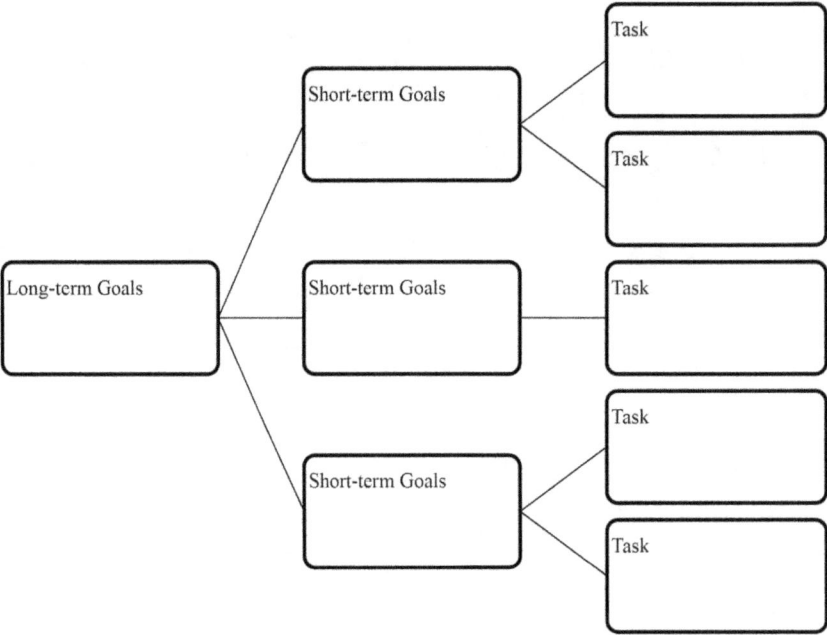

Figure 7.1a and b

National Science Teachers Association (NSTA), nsta.org

Teachers of English to Speakers of Other Languages (TESOL), tesol.org

Many of these associations have local or state chapters, and publish practitioner journals or magazines on a regular basis, many of which have significant national or state circulations. These journals or magazines have author instructions available online if you are unsure where to start.

You can also contact your local college or university. Many professors are rewarded for publishing outcome data from school programs, so they have a powerful incentive to assist you. They also could become an important partner and ally as you attempt to reach a broader audience.

Further, it is not difficult to be accepted to present your work at a regional, state, or even national conference. However, check the target audience of the conference first so you can be sure to reach the correct population (e.g., music teachers, school administrators). You may want to make sure your writing is clear and well organized and that you make a compelling case that your work is a good fit with the conference theme. Remember, it is a good thing to toot your own horn.

Finally, do not forget to keep rewarding yourself and to have fun! You deserve recognition for creating something new that benefits our youth, regardless of its scope. After all, isn't this why you got into teaching in the first place? Do not be surprised if you suddenly find yourself serving as a role model for other teachers wishing to expand their horizons. That is what this work is all about.

Appendix A

Sample Case 1—High School Reading Course

Case summary: Mr. Wayne is an urban high school special education teacher. He noticed that the only reading course available to struggling readers at his school focused on improving already-existing skills and did not address the needs of many of his students, who needed a beginning reading program. The reading levels of these students ranged from Pre-K to grade 3. How could Mr. Wayne create a structure in which students could earn credit and work at their skill level to improve their reading?

Outline Worksheet

Title of project: Skill-Based Reading Intervention One-sentence summary: This program will provide students struggling in reading (third-grade or below) with alternative learning materials based on skill level.
Goal The goal is to increase the skill level of reading fluency and reading comprehension among students struggling in reading whose current fluency levels are at the third-grade level or below.
Problem Thirty percent of students who are struggling in reading do not have learning material based on their skill level, because the current course targets those with third- through sixth-grade reading levels.

Solution
 	
- What (two sentences or less)
  Mr. Wayne will teach a resource class in reading intervention. He will pull students from their general education reading classes for half of their class periods.
 	
- When
  Thirty minutes per day, two to three times a week.
 	
- Where
  Mr. Wayne's resource room
 	
- Stakeholders
  General education reading teachers
  Principal
  Parents
  Students whose reading levels are at third grade or below
 	
- Costs
  Skill-based curriculum (e.g., Reading Mastery or Wilson Reading System)

Figure BM1.1

> Issues (n/a if not applicable)
>
> - Transportation n/a
>
> - Space n/a
>
> - Parent permission
>   Students' Individualized Education Plans (IEPs) will need to be modified with parent permission
>
> - Chain of approval
>   Principal→Parents
>
> - Evaluation (including progress monitoring)
>
> Curriculum-based measures will be developed; progress-monitoring fluency probes will be given every two weeks.

Figure BM1.1 1 (Continued)

Brainstorming Worksheet

Choice of formats: individual ☒ group ☐ both ☐

Justification for choice of formats:

Individuals such as the principal and fellow teachers will be adequate for planning the implementation of this intervention.

Preparation checklist

☒ Prepare written materials (e.g., agenda, timetable)

☒ Identify time and location Mr. Wayne's resource room (meeting with general and special education teachers); principal's office (meeting with principal)

☒ Objectives (list below)

   1. Determine procedure for identifying students
   2. Determine scheduling
   3. Locate appropriate materials

☒ Questions you want to be answered

   1. How should students be identified?
   2. What would the schedule look like?
   3. What assessments should be used (in addition to AimsWeb)?
   4. How much will new material cost, and how can funds be located to cover the cost?

☒ Locate thank-you gift $5 Starbucks card for teachers

☒ Write ground rules (for focus groups only)

   n/a

☒ List all materials (e.g., copies, chart paper, markers)

   Agenda listing questions and identifying target implementation date

   Laptop for note taking

Figure BM1.2

Box BM1.1: Preliminary Timeline Worksheet

Target implementation date: August 2017

Major tasks list

1. Conduct brainstorming sessions (general and special education teachers, principal and special education supervisor)
2. Identify curriculum
3. Identify students who meet criterion for inclusion in new program
4. Determine intervention schedule
5. Conduct IEP meetings with parents to obtain permission
6. Create instructional plan, including assessment

Appendix A

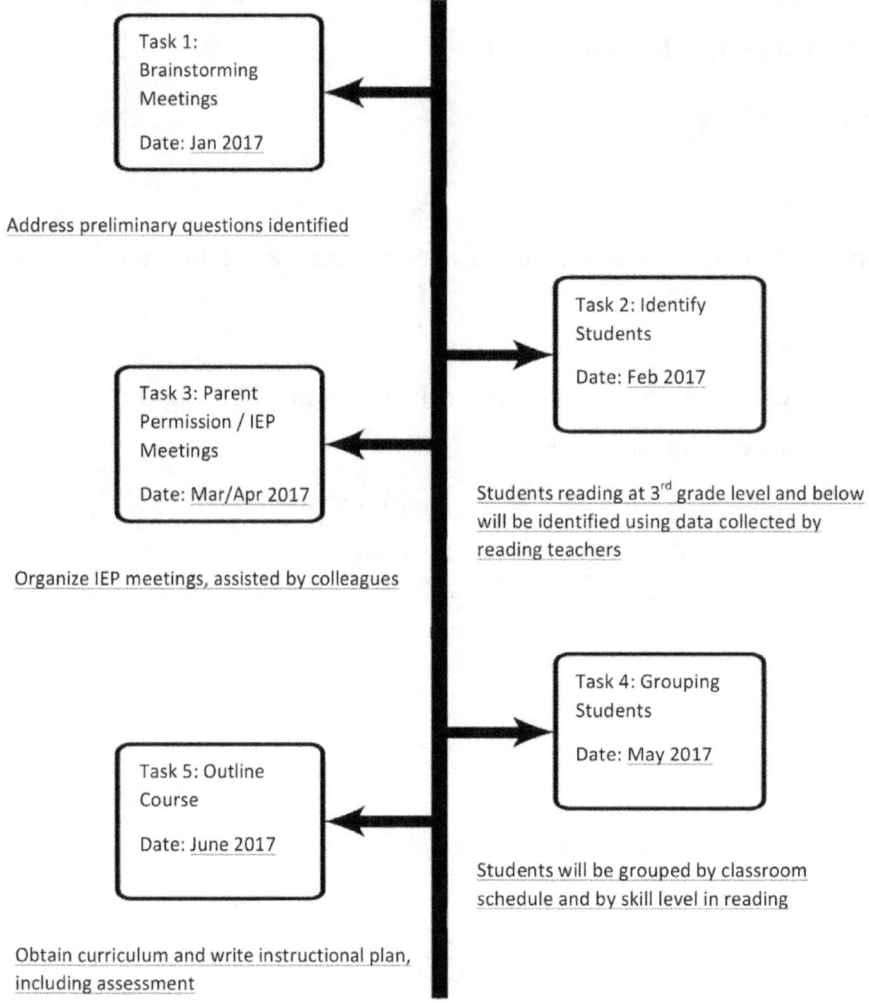

Table BM1.1

\multicolumn{4}{c}{*Evaluation Worksheet*}			
Goals	*Possible Outcomes*	*Data Sources*	*Logistics*
Students' reading fluency will improve	Improved fluency measurements and standardized test scores in fluency	Grades, curriculum-based measures (e.g., AimsWeb); state test scores in fluency	Probes will be administered weekly; standardized test annually
Students' reading comprehension will improve	Improved grades due to better understanding of material in numerous subjects	Grades, probes from easycmb.com	Probes will be administered monthly; grades measured quarterly
Increased student engagement	Increased school engagement due to improved reading ability	Shortened version of "High School Survey of Student Engagement" from Indiana University Center for Evaluation and Educational Policy (CEEP)	Students complete survey at beginning and end of semester

Proposal

Title of project: Skill-Based Reading Intervention

Your name: Mr. Wayne

Date: December 2, 2016

Project overview

> I noticed that approximately 30 percent of the students identified as needing reading intervention are reading at the third-grade level or below. Our current reading instruction does not target these students, all of whom have been identified as needing special services. I propose to provide a small group, skill-based reading intervention to these students as a pull-out service from their general education reading course.

Logistics

- Who? Students whose reading fluency scores are at 3.0 level or below
- What? Skill-based reading intervention targeting fluency and comprehension
- When? Thirty minutes per day, two to three times per week
- Where? My resource room
- How? I will provide a pull-out small group session during the general education reading course; I can fit two sessions into one class period

Evaluation: Students will be assessed on fluency and comprehension using curriculum-based measures. Standardized test scores and grades will also be analyzed.

Target implementation: August 2017

Next steps:

- Identify students placing at or below third-grade level in fluency
- Contact parents to schedule IEP meetings
- Identify curriculum

Potential challenges:

- Collaborating with general education teachers to align schedules and content
- Contacting parents and completing IEP meetings
- Funding for curriculum
- Scheduling

Figure BM1.4

Sample Case 1—High School Reading Course / 43

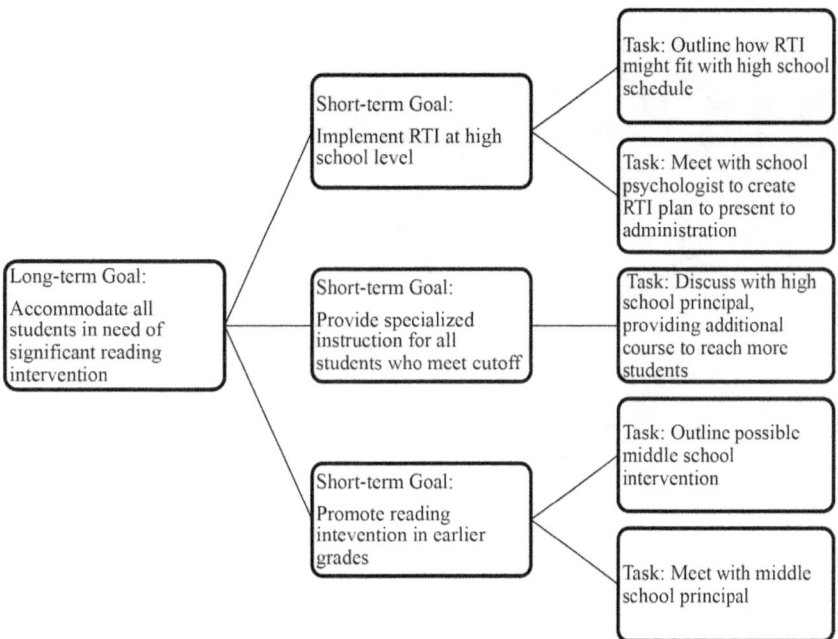

Appendix B

Sample Case 2—Middle-School Gifted Math Intervention

Case summary: A rural middle school implemented a fifty-minute tutorial block in the middle of the day so that students could obtain additional academic assistance in any area of need. However, the school quickly found that many students were not making optimal use of the tutorial.

Ms. Gilbert, a math teacher, realized that many of the students who were not using the tutorial period for learning activities were actually those students identified as gifted. Not needing any intervention, they were choosing to play on their district-assigned laptops instead of using the opportunity to get ahead in classwork and homework. How could Ms. Gilbert use the tutorial block to assist this group of gifted learners?

Outline Worksheet

Title of project: Mathematics Enrichment for Gifted Students

One-sentence summary:

Students identified as gifted will be provided with self-paced instruction in mathematics during tutorial block to support accelerated pacing and content enrichment.

Goal

Increase classroom engagement among gifted students during tutorial block, and increase mathematics achievement

---

Problem

Currently, all students, including gifted students, have been placed in a tutorial block in order to receive academic assistance. However, many of the gifted students have become disengaged because they do not need additional assistance with current coursework.

Solution

- What (two sentences or less)
  During the tutorial block, gifted students will receive mathematics enrichment.

- When
  Tutorial block

- Where
  Within current tutorial classrooms

- Stakeholders
  Tutorial teachers
  Gifted math teachers
  Principal
  Gifted coordinator
  Parents

- Costs
  The costs will include self-paced enrichment materials for gifted students as well as professional development for teachers.
  Issues (n/a if not applicable)

- Transportation
  n/a

Figure BM2.1

- Space
  n/a

- Parent permission
  Letters would be sent out to parents asking for permission to give their students additional enrichment during the tutorial block.

- Chain of approval
  General education teachers→Gifted coordinator→Principal

- Evaluation (including progress monitoring)
  Teacher rating scales on classroom engagement, mathematics achievement scores

Figure BM2.1 Continued

Brainstorming Worksheet

Choice of formats: individual ☐   group ☒   both ☐

Justification for choice of formats:

The school community will need to be on board and collaborate to implement this project, particularly since it is occurring in multiple classrooms.

Preparation checklist

☒ Prepare written materials (e.g., agenda, timetable)

☒ Identify time and location <u>3:15 in teachers' lounge</u>

☒ Objectives (list below)

    1. Identify target students and teachers (will need master schedule and class lists)
    2. Identify appropriate format and curriculum
    3. Determine logistics for professional development

☒ Questions you want to be answered

    1. Who will pilot this intervention (i.e., what teachers and students will be involved at the beginning)?
    2. What curriculum should be used?
    3. How will the intervention be structured?
    4. What reward system can be put in place to motivate students?
    5. What professional development will be needed?

☒ Locate thank-you gift <u>free sandwich from Subway</u>

☒ Write ground rules

    1. Avoid cell phones and side conversations
    2. Be encouraging and respectful of others' contributions

☒ List all materials (e.g., copies, chart paper, markers)

    1. Tutorial class rosters with gifted students highlighted
    2. Markers
    3. Whiteboard
    4. Summaries of potential curricula

Figure BM2.1

Box BM2.1: Preliminary Timeline Worksheet

Target implementation date: <u>September 2017</u>

Major tasks list

1. Conduct brainstorming session
2. Select evidence-based enrichment material
3. Determine what teachers/classrooms will pilot project
4. Obtain parent permission
5. Provide professional development for teachers
6. Determine structure for implementation in the classroom

Table BM2.1

	Timeline #1
Date: February 2, 2017	
March 2017	Task: Brainstorming meeting Where: JHS Who: Ms. Gilbert, with gifted coordinator, mathematics department chair, assistant principal Notes: See Brainstorming Worksheet
April 2017	Task: Complete selection of curriculum/materials Where: JHS Who: Ms. Gilbert, gifted coordinator Notes: Check available funds
April 2017	Task: Complete logistics Where: JHS Who: Ms. Gilbert Notes: Check master schedule, send parent letters, administer engagement surveys to targeted teachers and students
May 2017	Task: Professional development workshop Where: JHS during an in-service day Who: Curriculum specialist, teachers piloting intervention Notes:

Table BM2.2

Evaluation Worksheet			
Goals	Possible Outcomes	Data Sources	Logistics
Increase classroom engagement during tutorial	Improved attitude and behavior during tutorial block, increased focus on academics	Select instruments for teacher and student from this document*	Will need to administer engagement surveys during current year
Increase mathematics achievement	Better grades and test scores	Grades in mathematics classes, standardized test results (STAR test and state achievement test)	Grades collected quarterly, standardized test scores annually, will need to compare to previous achievement/scores

*IES National Center for Education Evaluation and Regional Assistance, Measuring Student Engagement in Upper Elementary through High School: A Description of 21 Instruments, http://ies.ed.gov/ncee/edlabs/regions/southeast/pdf/REL_2011098.pdf

Proposal

Title of project: Mathematics Enrichment for Gifted Students

Your name: Ms. Gilbert

Date: February 28, 2017

Brief overview

> Because many gifted students currently are disengaged during the tutorial block and do not need additional support in coursework, they will be provided with enrichment opportunities in mathematics in their tutorial classroom.

Logistics

- Who? Teachers of selected tutorial classes in which gifted students are placed
- What? Gifted students will be provided enrichment activities in mathematics
- When? During the tutorial block
- Where? Within the students' assigned tutorial classroom
- How? With parent permission and evidence-based learning material, teachers will guide the instruction of the gifted students in their classrooms

Evaluation: Pre- and post-measures of student engagement, grades in math classes, and scores on standardized tests will determine impact of intervention on class engagement and mathematics achievement.

Timeline: March—brainstorming; April—select materials, determine logistics; May—professional development for teachers piloting intervention.

Next steps: Brainstorming regarding format, curriculum, pilot classrooms, and students.

Anticipated costs: Selected learning material will be the primary cost of the intervention. The professional development workshop may be an additional cost.

Figure BM2.3

Table BM2.3

Growth and Development Plan #1			
Project title: Math Break!			
Goal	*Tasks*	*Targeted completion date*	*Notes*
Expand program to cover all tutorials that include gifted students	Determine logistics Discuss with teachers not participating in pilot	January 2018	Provide preliminary data
Goal	*Tasks*	*Targeted completion date*	*Notes*
Expand program to all interested students	Discuss with teachers who do not have gifted students in tutorial Survey all students regarding perceptions of Math Break! Create differentiation plan with curriculum specialist and general education math teachers	January 2019	Provide data to demonstrate success

Appendix C

Sample Case 3—Alternative School Program

Case summary: Mr. Meade, a middle-school teacher, saw a gap in at-risk education in his district. For years, he had been successful with taking eighth graders who had failed multiple middle-school classes in the past and given them the skills they needed to pass eighth grade. However, Mr. Meade found that once these students reached high school, their gains began to unravel. With no safety net in place and the environment of a large high school building, many of them began failing again.

Once they reached eleventh grade, these students had more options, such as work study and career/technical education, but many dropped out because of their lack of credits. As part of the intervention, Mr. Meade would like to make use of the large numbers of education majors at the local college who need hands-on experience working with high school students. What intervention could Mr. Meade create that would assist these students during their crucial ninth- and tenth-grade years?

Outline Worksheet

Title of project: Alternative School Project One-sentence summary: The Alternative School Project is a program that meets on the local college campus to provide additional support to ninth- and tenth-grade students transitioning to high school.
Goal The goal is to ensure that participating students have sufficient credits to be considered sophomores after their freshman year.
Problem Currently, about 5 percent of the school's freshmen are at risk for dropping out of school. This designation is made from eighth-grade student data, in terms of those students failing two or more courses, absent ten or more days, and with two or more behavior infractions. The school's history has shown that these students could potentially benefit from the work study or career/technical education made available in eleventh grade, but many do not have enough credits to be considered juniors by their third year. Some of those students later choose to drop out with insufficient opportunities to make up credits.
Solution <ul><li>What (two sentences or less) This project will be an alternative school program located on the local college campus.</li><li>When Half-day every day; morning session 7:30 to 11:00, afternoon session 12:00 to 2:30</li><li>Where Classroom TBD, Local University</li><li>Stakeholders Teachers Principal Parents and students University faculty University education majors</li><li>Costs School transportation for high school students</li></ul>

Figure BM3.1

Issues (n/a if not applicable)

- Transportation
  Consider whether this project can run simultaneously with other routes (e.g., high school students going to the college to study or work; special education job placement)

- Space
  University partners need to locate a classroom.

- Parent permission
  Parent permission is needed for the students participating in this program.

- Chain of approval
  Formal proposals must be presented to school district for approval for transportation; university attorney to approve students on campus; education dean to approve field placement.

- Evaluation (including progress monitoring)
  Grades, attendance, behavior, to be collected quarterly

Figure BM3.1 (Continued)

Brainstorming Worksheet

Choice of formats: individual ☐   group ☐   both ☒

Justification for choice of formats:

This is a complex partnership that involves both university and school personnel. Individual meetings with a Local U associate dean and the school's assistant principal should take place before a group meeting involving representatives from both partnering institutions. This format will allow for some of the details to be worked out in before coming together in partnership for a larger meeting.
Preparation checklist

☒ Prepare written materials (e.g., agenda, timetable)

☒ Identify time and location <u>Individual meetings in offices at THS and Local U; group meeting at potential site on Local U campus</u>

☒ Objectives (list below)

Individual	Group
1. Determine target population from THS and State U	1. Determine target population from THS and State U
2. Determine goals	2. Determine scheduling
3. Identify appropriate leadership team	3. Identify appropriate leadership team

☒ Questions you want to be answered

Individual	Group
1. Who will be involved in this project?	1. Who will be involved in this project?
2. What are the goals for each entity (THS and State U)?	2. How will the project be scheduled (times, classes offered)?
3. Who will oversee this project on each side?	3. Who will oversee this project on each side?

☒ Locate thank-you gift <u>$5 Starbucks gift card</u>

☒ Write ground rules

1. Rephrase "this cannot work" into a suggestion.

2. Refrain from using cell phones when possible.

3. Respect others' suggestions.

Figure BM3.2

> ☒ List all materials (e.g., copies, chart paper, markers)
> 1. Agenda (includes purpose of partnership, objectives, abbreviated timeline)
> 2. Copies of THS and Local U schedules
> 3. Markers
> 4. Chart paper

Figure BM3.2 (Continued)

Box BM3.1: Preliminary Timeline Worksheet

Target implementation date: August 2018

Major tasks list

1. Individual brainstorming session
2. Group brainstorming session
3. Complete proposals
4. Set up transportation
5. Finalize calendar and daily schedule
6. Identify classroom (Local U)
7. Set up classroom
8. Identify students
9. Establish curriculum
10. Obtain parent permission and notify selected students
11. Plan for data collection

Table BM3.1

Timeline #2		
Month	*Major Tasks*	*Minor Tasks*
September	Individual meetings at THS and Local U	Write up meeting summaries
October	Focus group	
November	Submit proposals	Check proposed location(s) at Local U
December		
January	Write tentative schedule	Locate permission slips
February	Meet with counselors Send out permission slips	
March	Meet with transportation	
April	Finalize schedule	Create one-page information sheet
May	Meet with combined leadership team to review logistics	Set up communication plan with THS teachers (who will have these students the other half-day)
June		
July	Set up classroom	
August	Implementation	

Table BM3.2

Evaluation Worksheet			
Goals	Possible Outcomes	Data Sources	Logistics
Improve credit attainment	Earn more credits than they would have otherwise obtained	Semester report cards	Will need comparison group to show improvement for ninth-grade students; for tenth-grade students, we can compare their performance to that of their ninth-grade year

> **Proposal**
>
> Title of project: Campus Mentors
>
> Your name: Mr. Meade
>
> Date: October 17, 2017
>
> Brief overview (one to two sentences)
>
> > This half-day program is designed to replace general education instruction for ninth- and tenth-grade students who are most at risk. These students will be identified by a team at THS and sent to Local U's campus to work with education majors as tutors or one-on-one mentors.
>
> Logistics
>
> - Who? Ninth- and tenth-grade students identified as at risk; education majors at Local U
> - What? Half-day credit-granting program taught by Mr. Meade
> - When? 7:30 to 11:00 am; 12:00 to 2:30 pm daily
> - Where? B. Hall at Local U
> - How? Mr. Meade will use online curriculum, aided by tutors and one-on-one mentors
>
> Evaluation: Semesterly report cards will measure GPA and credit attainment.
>
> Timeline: Target implementation August 2018
>
> Next steps:
>
> - Determine schedule
> - Identify qualifying students
> - Set up transportation
>
> Costs: THS student transportation
>
> Challenges:
>
> - Paying for transportation
> - Getting parents and students on board
> - Obtaining and setting up classroom at Local U
> - Setting up communication plan with THS teachers
>
> Growth and Development Plan #1

Figure BM3.3

Project title: Campus Mentors

Goal	Tasks	Targeted completion date	Notes
Expand campus connections/ student involvement	Use campus contacts to increase involvement	September 2019	Academic departments: Family Studies, Juvenile Justice, Nursing Organizations: Rec Sports Center, Campus Dining, Team/Club Sports, future teacher organizations
Goal	Tasks	Targeted completion date	Notes
Present data at state conferences	Collect and analyze data, write proposal	November 2019	Locate faculty partner to assist with data collection, analysis, write-up
Goal	Tasks	Targeted completion date	Notes
Expand model to additional sites	Send proposal to State U1 and State U2, and neighborhood schools	June 2020	Create one-page data summary, including quotes from students Send e-mail with summary, invite for site visit

Figure BM3.3 (Continued)

Appendix D

Sample Case 4—Arts Enrichment

Case summary: Ms. Sims, an elementary school art teacher, sees the need for additional services for her students. Because of district cutbacks, she is able to see each of the students in her school only for one thirty-minute block each week. Further, she has limited supplies and limited space to display her students' artwork.

Although Ms. Sims has the support of parents, the district simply cannot afford to hire another art teacher or spend more money on supplies. Many of her students display remarkable talent in art, but additional art instruction for children simply is not available in the community. How can Ms. Sims provide supplemental art instruction, given these limitations?

Outline Worksheet

Title of project: After-School Art Program One-sentence summary: A supplemental art program will be provided at the Local Arts Center after school on Tuesdays for interested students.
Goal Provide an opportunity for students to develop their artistic skill and expression.
Problem With limited supplies and space, students receive only thirty minutes a week in art class. This situation severely limits their opportunity to enhance and refine their artistic skills.
Solution - What (two sentences or less) An after-school art program - When Tuesdays after school, 4:00 to 5:00 pm. - Where Local Arts Center - Stakeholders School administration Local Arts Center Parents Students - Costs To be determined, include transportation and supplies
Issues (n/a if not applicable) - Transportation Transportation will be needed from school to Local Arts Center. - Space Local Arts Center is willing to donate space. - Parent permission Parent permission will be required for participation and transportation. - Chain of approval Arts Center→Principal→Parents - Evaluation (including progress monitoring) Use Goshen College's Art Rubric to assess artwork

Figure BM4.1

Brainstorming Worksheet

Choice of formats: individual ☐   group ☐   both ☒

Justification for choice of formats:

The principal and the Local Arts Center director will assist in determining the logistics of the project, but a group of artists and art teachers is necessary to assist in determining the content of the classes.

Preparation checklist

☒ Prepare written materials (e.g., agenda, timetable)

☒ Identify time and location <u>Individual meetings in offices; group meeting at Local Arts Center on Thursday after school</u>

☒ Objectives (list below)

Individual	Group
1. Determine logistics (when, where)	1. Determine curriculum
2. Discuss costs to parent	2. Determine assessment plan
3. Determine advertising plan	

☒ Questions you want to be answered

Individual	Group
1. What will the schedule look like?	1. What should be taught and how?
2. How much will parents need to pay?	2. How should progress be assessed?
3. How should the project be advertised?	

☒ Locate thank-you gift <u>$10 art supply store gift card for artists/art teachers only</u>

☒ Write ground rules

1. No cell phones
2. Focus on motivating all learners
3. Remain positive about possibilities

☒ List all materials (e.g., copies, chart paper, markers)

1. Agenda
2. Markers and chart paper
3. Notes from meetings with principal and Local Arts Center director
4. Notes on potential curricula

Figure BM4.2

Box BM4.1: Preliminary Timeline Worksheet

Target implementation date: September 2016

Major tasks list

1. Meet with principal and Local Arts Center director
2. Gather list of interested parents/students
3. Create curriculum map
4. Conduct focus group
5. Create flyer and parent letters/permission slips
6. Set up transportation
7. Gather supplies
8. Conduct research on other after-school art programs (goals, curriculum, evaluation)

Table BM4.1

Timeline #2		
Month	Major Tasks	Minor Tasks
January		
February		
March	Meet with principal and Arts Center director	Research other after-school arts programs
April	Conduct focus group; meet with interested parents	Gather materials for focus groups
May	Set up transportation	
June	Create curriculum map	
July	Gather supplies	Create permission slips
August	Send out permission slips at start of school	
September	Implementation	Collect permission slips; recruit teacher to locate students and ride the bus the first day
October		
November		
December		

Table BM4.2

Evaluation Worksheet			
Goals	*Possible Outcomes*	*Data Sources*	*Logistics*
Understand and apply elements and principles of design in personal works of art, utilizing a variety of media, tools, and processes (Indiana Academic Standards for Visual Arts)	Improve understanding and application of artistic principles	Goshen College "Art Rubric" art assessment, https://www.goshen.edu/art/ed/rubric2.html	Will need to conduct pre- and post-assessment; also use the work of students who do not participate in the program as a "control group"; consider multiple scorers

> **Proposal**
>
> Title of project: <u>Art Alive!</u>
>
> Your name: <u>Ms. Sims</u>
>
> Date: <u>May 2016</u>
>
> Brief overview (one to two sentences)
>
> > Because students currently are limited to thirty minutes a week for art class, this after-school art program will provide students with an additional opportunity to develop their artistic skills and interests.
>
> Logistics
>
> - Who? Students at Linnwood E.S.
> - What? After-school art program
> - When? Tuesdays 4:00 to 5:00 pm
> - Where? Local Arts Center
> - How? Transportation will be provided from Linnwood to Local Arts Center. Parents will pick up at 5:00 pm.
>
> Evaluation:
>
> Timeline: First class to be held September 20, 2016; permission slips due September 9
>
> Next steps
>
> - Set up transportation
> - Create curriculum map
> - Gather supplies
>
> Cost to parents: Transportation and supplies (approximately $70 per student per ten-week session)
>
> Challenges: Providing quality program with limited budget; locating funding for students on free/reduced lunch

Figure BM4.3

Table BM4.3

Growth and Development Plan #1			
Project title: Art Alive!			
Goal	Tasks	Targeted completion date	Notes
Expand number of seats available	Use Local Arts Center Tuesdays and Thursdays	January 2017	Students will pick one day per week; discuss with Local Arts Center
Goal	Tasks	Targeted completion date	Notes
Locate donor for supplies	Meet with Arts Council; apply for grants	Summer 2017	Need strategy to locate donors; also try local businesses that support the arts
Goal	Tasks	Targeted completion date	Notes
Locate permanent display for Art Alive! artwork	Conduct brainstorming session	September 2017	Focus group will be asked to think creatively about local spaces
Goal	Tasks	Targeted completion date	Notes
Include all elementary schools in district	Discuss with principals; expand partnership	September 2018	Will need additional teachers; consider cooperative with local artists

About the Author

Leah Wasburn-Moses is professor of educational psychology at Miami University. She was formerly a special education teacher at Jefferson High School in Lafayette, Indiana, where she began an in-school tutoring program for struggling readers. She is director of Campus Mentors, alternative schools targeting youth at risk located on college campuses, and FreeTeacher U, an alternative teacher licensure apprenticeship in special education.